Virtue, Big as Sin

Frank Osen's *Virtue, Big as Sin* offers one witty, elegant poem after another. The rhymes are especially clever, the meter sure, the stanzas well-shaped, but this poet's sense of proportion is also reflected in wisdom (and what is wisdom but a sense of proportion?). An urbane maker of sparkling phrases like "that genuine Ur of the ersatz," Osen can also write plainly, movingly, about a young girl's funeral. And he reflects often on art itself, which he so rightly calls "the conjured awe."
—Mary Jo Salter (Judge, 2012 Able Muse Book Award)

Reading *Virtue, Big as Sin* has left me with the sense of satisfaction and enduring pleasure that really good poetry always produces, even when it also does the rest of what honest writing may do: confirm suspicions about ourselves we wish we could refute, bring to mind aspects of nature we'd rather forget, and deliver alarming news about the future, both public and private. Frank Osen does all of this and much more, all with grace and wit, in language that makes the messenger thoroughly "one of us."

The poems move without apparent effort from pantoum to free verse, from senryu-like short forms to het-met surprises, to numerous and marvelous variations on the sonnet, many of them as "surreptitious" as the one devoted to a journal entry by Wallace Stevens. The same assured, unobtrusive mastery of prosody is evident in Osen's use of puns—sometimes in layers!—and ekphrasis; in his use of dreams, as in "Tell," and his direct address, often to the absent, and most movingly to the dead; and in the kind of "framed memory" approach that allows an aging man, in poem after poem, to recognize, without distortion or pity, the youth he was.

The poet's extraordinary imagery includes the kind of deliberate visual play that takes the reader with him into error and its resolution, as in "Distant Pipes," into the joys and challenges of craftsmanship, as in "Refinishing Weather," and into metaphysical speculation, as in that perfect example of extended metaphor, "The Lath House," whose slowly expanding sense never quite hardens into a fixed, finished insight, but seems, rather, "designed to never seem quite finished." I'm tempted to say that the poems I've named are, all by themselves, worth the entire book, but no, those others—the humorous ones, both light and dark, and the descriptions, such as "Chant of the Artifact," that give the reader's inner eye a new capacity for observation—are all important parts of the whole that no reader would want to lose.

I want to close by mentioning two that moved me especially because, like the poet, I am a parent and know something about the anxiety he conveys obliquely in both: "Spinning Out," in which the speaker, waiting for his teenaged son to take his driver's exam, remembers a stupid risk he himself once took behind the wheel, but now recalls with a degree of clarity—and horror—not available to him when he was young and childless; and finally, "We Go Without You," in which the speaker attends the funeral of a friend's child and ends up wishing his own absent but very-much-alive daughter an unexpected kind of luck.

Poems like these exhibit the clarity, depth and universality that allows some texts to last and keep the reader company for life. This is not always the case for contemporary poetry though it may initially seem more stylish or shocking.
—Rhina P. Espaillat

Frank Osen's poems revel in beauty and pleasure, in technical dexterity and high-gloss finish. Readers who care about such things will be abundantly rewarded. But the reveling is haunted by loss, awful possibilities of failure, a nothingness glimpsed beneath the carnival. One of Osen's avowed tutelary spirits is Wallace Stevens, and his probing of his subjects can often seem like an extended, heart-wrenching commentary on Stevens's line, "Death is the mother of Beauty." The fragility of beauty, the omnipresence of death, and the intimate connections between them, are everywhere present in these marvelously heartening and effective poems.
—Dick Davis

In his talent for tragedy and comedy, and for mixing them, Osen takes his place in a distinguished line of English-language poets that runs from Chaucer and Shakespeare down to our day.
—Timothy Steele (full text in the afterword)

Virtue, Big as Sin

POEMS BY

Frank Osen

WINNER OF THE 2012 ABLE MUSE BOOK AWARD

ABLE MUSE PRESS

Able Muse Press

www.ablemusepress.com

Printed in the United States of America

Library of Congress Control Number: 2013932425

ISBN 978-1-927409-16-9 (paperback)
ISBN 978-1-927409-17-6 (digital)

Cover image: "Letting Go" by Anja Bührer

Cover & book design by Alexander Pepple

Able Muse Press is an imprint of *Able Muse:* A Review of Poetry, Prose & Art—at www.ablemuse.com

Able Muse Press
467 Saratoga Avenue #602
San Jose, CA 95129

With all my love, to Susan,
Lauren, Hayley, and Robert.

And to Lynn Osen, who dedicated *Women in Mathematics*
to me in 1974, a dedication in return.

Acknowledgments

I am grateful to the editors of the following journals where many of these poems originally appeared, sometimes in earlier versions.

14 by 14: "The Switches."

Able Muse: "Ligan."

American Arts Quarterly: "Portrait of Alexis Piron [?]."

The Chimaera: "The Pursuit," "Tell."

Comstock Review: "Distant Pipes."

The Dark Horse: "Private School."

The Evansville Review: "The Lath House."

First Things: "Unawares, by Parrots."

The Flea: "Mindful."

Light Quarterly: "Samuel Johnson and the Poets' Corner."

Lucid Rhythms: "At the Dedication of von Weber's Monument in Dresden, October 11, 1860," "Misfortunes of Juan Crisóstomo Jacobo Antonio de Arriaga y Balzola."

Measure: "Medicine Cabinet."

Per Contra: "Abstaining."

POOL: "Penelope's Shield."

The Raintown Review: "November Flea Market," "Pacific Drift," "Refinishing Weather," "Reproof."

The Rotary Dial: "We Go Without You," "Yards," "Spinning Out," "Hymn Outside a Bank," "Potemkin Village Idiot."

The Shit Creek Review: "Going Amis."

Snakeskin: "Focus."

Soundzine: "Two-Person Ketch."

The Spectator: "Tube Station, Jubilee Line," "Forget Not Yet," "On a Competition."

The Susquehanna Quarterly: "Cover Memo," "Under the Lighthouse."

Think Journal: "Chant of the Artifact."

Unsplendid: "Study."

The Wallace Stevens Journal: "So Noble That . . . "

I am grateful to the organizers of the following contests where the corresponding listed poems placed: "Distant Pipes," winner, 2008 *Eratosphere* Deck the Halls competition; "Medicine Cabinet," finalist, 2006 Howard Nemerov Sonnet competition; "Penelope's Shield," winner, 2008 *Best American Poetry* series poem award; "Refinishing Weather," first runner-up, 2008 Morton Marr Poetry prize; "Reproof," fourth place, 2010 *Writers Digest* competition; "Yards," finalist, 2012 Morton Marr Poetry prize.

Contents

PART 3   *SUSTAINING SOUND*

Virtue, Big as Sin

PART 1   *CONDUITS*

Chant of the Artifact

Whisper *stick and stone and string.*
The implement has now been polished.
It quivers like a living thing
that skill endowed and age demolished.

The implement has now been polished—
though remnant of another time
that skill endowed and age demolished—
while hidden as a playground rhyme.

Though remnant of another time,
chords still ghost through wood and stone,
while hidden as a playground rhyme:
What bound the knot that knit the bone?

Cords still ghost through wood and stone,
whisper, *stick and stone and string,*
what bound the knot that knit the bone?
It quivers like a living thing.

Pacific Drift

We're on the brambled slope above your house
and I'm still gazing west to Catalina,
where the horizon's shortly going to douse
an undulant, impossibly pink sun.
Sailboats are sifting north to the marina;
Laguna's pastel patch beyond that palm
is like a master watercolor done
in an eponymous pacific calm.

Four years ago, it was a different story:
earthmovers shifted all this rise away,
and evenings, you were on the phone to me,
complaining that your place looked like a quarry.
The county called you, though, it was okay;
they'd shore, restore, and pay you for your trouble,
but still, it hurt you somewhere deep to see
a once-imposing height come down to rubble.

Support has never been my strongest suit.
I tend to bulldoze things; I'd scoff and say
your lot was not as stable as it seemed,
what good were vistas that could slip away?
No purchase you had here was absolute;
you knew unanchored places often slid;
you'd have replacements that you'd never dreamed.
And by degrees, within a year, you did.

You drifted downward; evening's fretfulness
became upheavals of late afternoon
(I'd yet to learn the doctors' term, *sundowning*).
A home of quite another sort came soon,
erosion of more faculties and girth,
a sliding towards complete forgetfulness
from which you'd sometimes call, like someone drowning
without a footing in familiar earth.

At sunsets, not so long ago, you'd stand
out on that terrace, raise a toast and note
how man-made fine particulates enhance
these evening skies; so when I've drunk my fill,
in awkward mimicry, I raise my hand
and let the bagful of your ashes float
through placid twilight, to the land's expanse.
It's fitting you'll become your newborn hill.

Medicine Cabinet

The opened door discloses dental floss
and nostrums for inducing sleep/zip/zoom
and there in the apothecary dross,
some pills I scavenged from your final room.
I gathered by the single word you wrote
across their quartered envelope, these might
produce a gentle deliquescent float,
if taken with a beer or two some night.

It always stops me, though, your ghostly hand:
four palsied letters skittered out in ink
that seem to waft in from another land.
Much stranger than an agonist, I think,
with so much else of you now laid to rest,
to find your *pain* at home inside my chest.

Portrait of Alexis Piron [?]

On a painting by Louis Tocqué

Though a Tiepolo commands the hall
(*Nobility and Virtue*, big as sin)
and nude Pomona drew me to this wall,
it's your averted gaze that draws me in.
Faced wrong-ways from her bounty, your displeasure
rakes door and docent both in equal measure.

But you were always good at misdirection.
Though patrons here would neither know nor care,
your plays were masterpieces of deception,
yours was the wit that flayed the famed Voltaire
so cleverly he sometimes missed its chafe,
and so condemned you always, to be safe.

No characters of yours are who they seem,
your dramas prize illusion, the false clue;
identities get cast off in midstream.
I check the name again; so, is this you?
Down to the question mark, that's Piron, pure,
to let us know we shouldn't be too sure.

Private School

The children driven out or off to bed,
I laze awhile in front of the TV,
half-noting how a half-familiar head
that's floating through a documentary
recalls my fifth grade teacher, Señor Rey,
a cartoon Argentinian: pomade,
a pencil moustache, and a pompous way
more suited to review a troop parade
than tutor lousy students through *Preguntas;*
his Spanish class devolved to dirty war.

Our side was good at engineering juntas
to oust his civil nature—we'd keep score.
So much for rulers whacked or cracked or broken,
a bonus, if the "army speech" got spoken:
I doo not want (his hands, assaying figs)
to bee a soldier (jack-knife with each wrist),
but (fingers pop like quickly kindled twigs)
I was a sergeant (here, the iron fist)
and if that's what you neeed, that's what I'll bee!

I'm watching now, while from a balcony
more distant still, an ancient despot spits
and slams the air. We young, self-styled *Maquis*—
what shits we were, what rotten little shits.
We won, the day we made the man atone
with stories of his vanished home, with tears

and curses—for the generals and Perón.
I push a button, and he disappears.
That, though, is what the unskilled tyrants do.
The defter ones are always tracing you.

Distant Pipes

Inked from Hiroshige's un-inked mist,
      rain-washed ridge
     and blank-imprinted bridge,
   sedge hat pulled down against a storm,
sleeves billowing beyond each outthrust fist,
     the figure bears its form.

Leaning, perhaps against divesting wind
      whose vanished track
     has stripped its staff and pack,
   the vision stands, as though resolved
to dare a thinning image further thinned,
     a floating world dissolved.

The ghostly image might be of some monk
      or Edo traveler,
     until—its own unraveler—
   it settles in a new arena:
as drainage pipes amid a drift of junk,
     roadside, in Pasadena.

It did this sleight-of-hand just once, then showed
      how any art
     might dazzle and impart
   its tricks (they brought me back to view
these conduits)—the conjured awe, the road
     we take to make them new.

Reproof

Up north today to catch a college game,
I'm nodding through the running commentaries
of friends recounting all our halt and lame,
when one says you're still hanging out at Perry's.
So afterwards, I go; it's not that far
and sure enough, beyond a row of beers
and spirits, and across a host of years,
your twenty-something picture tends the bar.

It's held its own, if not intensified—
that shock of blond, blue-eyed, electric poise,
worn since by countless Abercrombie boys
but current now, as on the night you died.
It's kept your image on that wall, iconic,
where memory and snapshot might concur
that at some other point in time, you *were*—
but memory blurs and adds its own laconic,

And then, you weren't—the accident, that spring
you worked here, fresh from school, was all your fault
and no surprise; we'd seen how you'd assault
the hills in your MG—a driven thing.
At least you never dreamed that you would maim

somebody, let alone the crash would claim
in slower motion, but every bit as wild,
your parents, who had lost their only child.

Now, gray as they were, past the young bud's day-
long grief and past a meaningless bouquet
and valedictory words, I stand composed
as an absurdly late eyewitness, posed
with, if not yours, still no one else's face
here in this fine and private public place.
I feel the impact like a passerby:
to know you're dead, but see you've yet to die.

Study

Brought to the deep end of the Afghan rug,
beyond the agapanthus-patterned chair,
she sees a tranquil lake of lacquer table
on which, today, admonitory ferns
nod above a hammered-copper kettle

and reflected in orange metal, the upward sweep
of an imagined arch, an intimation
of the virgin in a shadowed nook
above an empty cockle-fluted font.
Then, past red doors, a rough of brilliant sun

consumes an outside courtyard whole
but coolly bathes a little chapel's walls
in infantine and underwater pinks.
Mosaic floors (how many hadals deep?)
run rings of yellow brass that band

the kettle's bottom like a diving sphere,
easing in a stir of lamp-lit silt
through corals, to a sudden columned curtain
of applause, beyond which sits an audience
awaiting, on what stage, which matinee?

Where, for a moment now, she finds herself
disturbed that she's forgotten how to say.

Focus

It's not as if she saw him there
but backed her car and didn't care
or crept on when she heard him yell.
Still, he gives her holy hell.
She's agent of a greater fear:
a world that doesn't know he's here.

Under the Lighthouse

Her childhood headlands held a bay like glass,
commanded by a pleasant house and tower
of eaves and brick and sea-patinaed brass,
whose beacon seemed to shine with kindly power.

Lighthouses lost a few romantic gables
when she discovered that they worked like clocks;
their lamps revolved by counterweights and cables
that ran grandfather-wise, from top to ground.
And souls at sea might founder on the rocks
if tenders let the houses come unwound.

A keeper couldn't sleep on-shift at night.
That rule, however, could be circumvented
by napping underneath the lead half-ton
that lowered slowly from beneath the light.
Then, when you felt its pressure on your chest
you scrambled up, rewound, refueled, and tended
to all the work that needed to be done.
And so, in fits and starts, you got your rest.

She kept some memories of amber beams;
they seemed to dim, though, after she awoke
to oceans of responsibilities.
And now, for her, the night-tossed seas evoke
a figure, who's supine but apprehending
distant cries and dark catastrophes,
and always from above, a weight descending.

Yards

I knew a man once, who walked off a cliff.
That first night in our starter home, not sleeping—
things needed so much up-, or just safe-keeping—
we seemed to teeter on a steep What-If

the lawn should parch, the plaster crack, walls rot
into their timbers, tumble down? I felt
the tyranny of things our getting got,
was now our lot. Our neighbor wore a belt

of tools, as if to hammer home that fact,
which he did capably, each weekend-long
to sounds of projects driven, nailed and tacked,
or quartered to a table saw's loud song.

We verbed his name. To *Trimble:* plane a log
for drawer pulls; gild the undersides of eaves;
not merely rake, but marshal all the leaves
and—God! That saw—what's left to saw? The dog?

His calm and measured puttering, not reckless,
appeared designed to make us feel more feckless
in our hilarity of disrepair.
So one day, when he stepped off into air

while hiking, fell partway down a mountainside
and looked up at his daughter with a laugh,
and then (unused to doing things by half,
perhaps) rolled down the rest of it and died,

it seemed as if he'd planned and built a way
as sure as with an augur and a gauge,
to show how he could, on a Saturday,
do what might take some people half an age.

Tell

I dreamt I met our buddy Ted,
who asked what news I had to tell
and grinned to hear I'm on the mend
and better, since I married you.
He roared when I pronounced him fit
and said I hadn't changed a bit.
To quirky visions, ever true!
But then he told me, as my friend,
that he had died, you never wed,
and I am very far from well.

Cover Memo

Engaged at the office all day on a sonnet—surreptitiously.
— Wallace Stevens, journal entry, August 3, 1906

To: Distribution
                        Stevens was aware
that many poets must go leopard-like
among the striped but not be spotted there.

This isn't easy, when desire may strike
at work, although it called in sick last night,
and, stricken, one must chase in search of tea
or oils or oranges to some distant height—
or only to the nearest *OED*.

Yet when protective coloration's risked,
a job transcends that mental game preserve
where fauna don't go frolic, but get frisked.

For all who bear an office to observe,
we ought to mark each August third this way:
as annual Surreptitious Sonnet day.

Two-Person Ketch

Two novice sailors, *terra incognita,*
for so it was, and so we were, at sea,
just wed, our rented boat off Punta Mita.

The sail unreefed, we tilted hard alee
and hugged the weather rail until some sound
caused me to stand aslant and scan around,
not feeling how your hands had wrapped my waist
but sensing (if such things could ever be,
that then they would) a siren called to me.
I found then, how your arms held me embraced
and how you smiled, as if you hadn't heard,

or heard much better, singing of a sort.
I leaned to you, we kissed without a word
and brought our righted craft about, to port.

At the Dedication of von Weber's Monument in Dresden, October 11, 1860

Schaut, o schaut

— Der Freischütz

The tomb is built; they've promised to unveil
your statue here despite the rain. Now dead
some thirty years, but punctual without fail
and witty to your last, you might have said
your luck was always late, so it's not wrong
      but fitting that it's taken us this long.

Fitting, too, that the road was hard and rocky.
When friends first sought to bring your body home
from England, we protested—would Morlacchi
and *Kapellmeisters* in each catacomb
around the world, now have to be returned?
      We couldn't pay to have them all un-urned.

But now, the Court has come, and your son Max, on
whom you bestowed the name that Baron shares
with *Free-Shot*'s hero, is the perfect Saxon
atop the tribune there, and your affairs
merit this pomp and royal presence. Note,
      the iron cross at every other throat.

We've traipsed, I think, a little past the gate,
into those haunted woods you painted for us,
where evils worse than Zamiel may await
a nation not yet born, to sing its chorus
and harrow us with more than drums and strings,
        though it's not safe for clerks to think such things.

The speeches show no promise, yet, of ending.
To fight the damp, I conjure Black Hunt's theme,
entwining it with Agatha's, contending
my horn against the winds. The latter seem
augmented, though; I like your version better
        for here, they're harsher, colder, and much wetter.

At last, your grandson pulls the cord; I see
the sculptor, Rietschel, caught your likeness well.
Its mien is querulous and willowy
and, like your pieces, works a rending spell
that pulls my thought to thoughts even more spare,
        of man, transcendent as a sound in air.

The loved one's cry that fate tears him away,
as it did you, embarked with *Oberon*
for double grief—a grinding death, Planché—
all but that final magic bullet gone
and, as we know, the last one goes askew;
        it ends your darkest work, and ended you.

Although you must have sensed the worst, you went
to battle fools, to wreck your hope and health,
quite willing that your capital be spent,
not on yourself, but on your family's wealth.
How noble, how unequal, what mischance;
      you were the perfect father of romance.

You persevered with great ability,
aware there's no assurance that one's gifts
will free one's work from mediocrity.
I hear that in your music, and it lifts
my fear that art is wasted in one's labor;
      that's what I'd have you play for us, von Weber.

You, who now stand in Dresden at its wettest,
whose road here was circuitous and long,
knew when life proves one's most inept librettist,
one has to pair it with one's strongest song.
That was your truest shot across the glen,
      and now it opens up my heart again.

Mindful

I try imagining the earth I'll be,
but find I can't un-animate a plot—
can't help but swell a hill beside the sea
with canyon oak, the odd forget-me-not,

perhaps some cars to carve a road below,
running up the coast and out of sight
past distant cities throwing alpenglow
beneath a tiny, rising blip of light

that pulses brighter as it climbs the sky,
massaging contours into continents,
reporting from its one unwavering eye,
what passes for a world's intelligence.

It's made to span the whole it spins around,
and bound to spin until it comes to ground.

Ligan

Such a parcell of goods as the Mariners in a danger of
shipwracke cast out . . . and fasten to them a boigh . . .
that so they may find them, and have them againe . . .
are called . . . ligan

— *Les Termes de la Ley*

Storms will wrack, rocks can rend,
and even crueler calms rescind
the quick directives of the wind.
Any passing tide may blend

or swallow all the evidence,
so later, coming on the lines,
they're all that's left to give the sense
she ran the gale but read the signs,

and terrified she'd sink or burn,
hands made fast and cast adrift—
buoyant, blazoned like a gift—
a surety toward some return

to people on a peaceful quay.
Make light about the ends of rope,
but should you founder on the sea,
look where it marks and harbors hope.

PART 2   *SOME SAME, BETTER PLACE*

Potemkin Village Idiot

On the myth of authenticity

It grew in fame, as such things often do,
because it hits us where we live—a place
of neat facades one might construct on cue

to gull the gullible, and then un-brace
and rearrange, so that it's always fronting
some new, intriguingly familiar face.

Though scholars claim real buildings wore real bunting,
the false-front legend leaves us more to love.
Today, on Guadalupe beach, I'm hunting

a plaster sphinx and plywood remnants of
a movie set that Cecil B. DeMille
junked somewhere in the drifting dunes above.

How long before, near some Crimean hill,
a hyperrealist Russian oligarch
who's backed extensive excavations will

announce a find or new amusement park;
if not that genuine Ur of the ersatz,
re-re-re-resurrected from its dark

of moldered paperboard and rotted slats,
then an authentic, gleaming replication,
complete with rides and characters in hats?

I'd buy a ticket to that dedication
and souvenirs from each concessionaire,
but be compelled to tell the congregation

more times than anyone nearby could bear—
it's not the place that really wasn't there.

Tube Station, Jubilee Line

The smell's annoying and the noise is loud;
it sports graffiti here and there beneath
its coats of city grit—and that's the crowd
who've rushed or trudged to fill the gleaming sheath.

It takes off in a hush of whirring metal.
Across the aisle, one glum old gent, alone,
ignores our bright bough's freshest, wettest petal,
a girl who's just been jilted via phone.

But when she sobs, his handkerchief is offered;
her seatmate, who'd been buried in her map,
says, "He's not worth it, dear." A hug is proffered.
We also serve, who only mind the gap

and light her way with smiles at Southwark station.
As someone's cell phone plays "Amazing Grace,"
I almost feel we've all earned dispensation
and may arrive at some same, better place.

Abstaining

Quite late the morning after, Common Sense
regains the floor and moves a resolution:
Henceforth, this fractious body drinks no more!
The Hand that poured, now shakily relents;
the chastened Wits agree in mute confusion;
a turncoat Tongue and reddened Eyes implore
concurrence. As the motion carries, cheers
and ringing sounds continue in the Ears.

In all the din, none note a braying snore,
nor see, collapsed in perfect dissolution,
the instigator of their late offense,
who led the party-of-the-night-before.
He sleeps the session through without intrusion,
aware his comrades often jump the fence.
His slumber is untroubled: as Desire,
he'll speak tonight, though—and he'll be on fire.

Painter of Light

Here is the most pernicious piece of kitsch:
a candy-colored, vaguely Cotswold cottage,
confected to its mullioned windows, which
are spewing high-lit lights of unreal wattage,
"editioning devices," hand-applied
as extras by their marketeer, whose mills,
which mass-produce these images, must hide
just out of sight, beyond the livid hills.

Shadows don't dim its opalescent cheer.
This might be post-mod mocking at its worst,
except the composition seems to crow
don't change your life, just make believe you're here.
Or that's my second take on it. My first
was to draw, moth-like, toward its amber glow.

Forget Not Yet

A Dear John from a love poet

Forget not yet how we have striven,
though many times our hearts were riven,
through fights and breakups, all forgiven,
forget not yet.

Forget not yet our milder days,
before you seemed to change your ways,
your doctor says it's just a phase,
forget not yet.

Forget not yet the night I went
to pay your bail, the money spent;
they said you'd loitered with intent.
Oh, hell. Forget.

Samuel Johnson and the Poets' Corner

Johnson, though famously witty and crabby,
once failed to be either or get the last word:
with Oliver Goldsmith, at Westminster Abbey,
he'd paused in the corner where bards are interred.

He finally murmured with eye fixed afar,
Would our names might be found here, with those of our peers!
Then the two resumed walking to old Temple Bar,
where the heads of poor wretches sat rotting on spears.

Said Goldsmith, who knew what caprice often sends,
And our heads not be found here, with those of our friends.

So Noble That . . .

Exposing a tawdry joke at the bottom of "Mrs. Alfred Uruguay" by Wallace Stevens

The later Stevens built his own Parnassus
of towering poems, forbidding and austere.
It's not a place for jokes on tits and asses—
so why is Mrs. U. appearing here?

The sun goes down—so what, the moon, she's full—
upon this refugee from some soirée,
who's elegant, in velvet not in wool.
One senses that she wants to get away.

She commandeers a donkey, rides uphill
and past a horseman riding down—the end.
Who was it? (Virile Youth.) His horse? (All Will.)
How noble was that rider round the bend?

It's Stevens, the *lecteur* and *philosophe*,
who asks these questions, but it is his other—
old Wally, that insurance-fellow oaf—
who prompts the reader, finally, toward another:

This horseman guy meets Mrs. Uruguay
high on a mountain, gowned as for a dance,
astride a donkey, and does what?
                              Rides by
and never gives her ass a backwards glance.

Penelope's Shield

Laughing Boy returns and the dog drops dead.
Odysseus, did you think I wouldn't know?
Under this shroud
I've borne more absences than yours.
So what, if summer shared our golden bed?
Every winter wears the same disguise.

Growth and loss
loom larger with me, now—
urging weaves both ways,
casting my work in the sun's or fire's light—
knit with disciplined undoing.

Alcuin's Nightingale

From the Latin of Alcuinus

The hand that took you from my holly tree
in envy, stole a happiness from me.
You filled my heart with nature's sweetest words
and sang my soul the poetry of birds,
for which, let every creature winging air
attend and hymn with me in my despair.
Drab bird, whose tune wore such a sprightly coat
and spread abroad from such a narrow throat,
your song, in all its varied, rhythmic hues
was glory to creation and the Muse.
Unfailingly, in darkness, you'd rejoice
to heaven with a bright and sacred voice.
Should all the angels boom in praise of thunder,
once one had heard you, it would be no wonder.

Going Amis

Look your worst on all things always,
lovely, shitty, in between,
lovely tending ever fouler,
fouler growing evergreen,

how Bechet begot Gillespie,
then shag-bag mobs at their guitars.

Collect your final hugs and kisses,
strew the hay, reserve a hearse.
Odd, it's only time for going,
once there's no comfort left in knowing
that every bit as bad as this is,
each future iteration's worse.

On a Competition

I had just given in, tossed my works in a bin,
when this Wednesday some contest proclaimed one
fifth-best pastoral ode on a bodily node.
I'm a poet again, an acclaimed one.

I retract all my slurs on those once-tin-eared curs,
since the judge now esteems unsurpassed rhyme.
On my efforts Miltonic, she's smiled, solomonic—
she's so vastly improved since the last time.

Pour the finest cuvée, what a glorious day,
though I never once doubted I'd do it;
lesser poets can all sip their wormwood and gall
as they read it and covet and rue it.

I'm a maker, a seer, I'm a bard without peer,
with this win I'll have vanquished defeat, it
is a palpable joy I'd find quite unalloyed
if I thought I could ever repeat it.

PART 3   *SUSTAINING SOUND*

Misfortunes of Juan Crisóstomo Jacobo Antonio de Arriaga y Balzola

Va, les maux qui sont mon partage,
Ton cœur un jour les connaîtra.
— *Mercure de France* (Volume 38)

    Consider, first, that he was born a Basque,
one of those peoples whose collective task
is to ensure that they are not forgotten—
and, on that score alone, his luck was rotten.
He burned as hot and bright as Mozart, save,
young Amadeus's fame survived the grave.
The galloping consumption that consumed
a younger Juan Crisóstomo, entombed
his fame, as well. A friend sent home a trunk
with Juan's life work, which, on the journey, shrunk
      to what the rats and mice had judged inedible.

    Consider, next, that wandering regrettable
memorial tablet in Bilbao, which sat
at Calle de la Ronde and noted that
Arriaga had been born there: fifty years,
it took to place it and, as it appears,
another twenty-five to see its error—
for he'd been born on Calle *(¡ai!)* Somera.
Delayed, misplaced. Nor did the mordant joke
      end there: the tablet, when they moved it, broke.

For final evidence of fate's caprice,
consider Arriaga's final piece.
The tale of Hagar, sacrificial lamb
of Genesis and slave to Abraham,
who, banished to the desert with her son,
cries out against the wrong that has been done,
until the Lord directs her to a well
by which she saves the tribe of Ishmael.
Such might have been its end, had Arriaga
lived long enough to finish his cantata.
As with his life, though, *Agar* is too brief.

Ishmael awakens; in his thirst and grief,
he weeps and begs his mother for a drink.
There's none, they're left on an eternal brink.
She takes his hand and curses over him
in notes of pathos, unredeemed and grim,
Your hearts shall feel this evil hurt's division....
No providence completes the composition.
So Arriaga gave us, to his cost,
the truest lamentation of the lost.

Lines on a Rescue Fly Trap

He hangs it from a branch of flowering plum,
adds water and *voilà,* here's instant hell.
The little plastic bag begins to hum
with customers who soon show up in swarms,
until what's even ranker than the smell
and stays that way is the transparency.
For grotesque metaphor, it outperforms
old sermons on the price of errancy.

In fact, it's like a panel out of Bosch:
lured by desire for filth, drawn down a chute,
new flies arrive to join the seething mosh
in frantic flight above a lake of dead.
Some stay outside (perhaps the more astute)
and mark their lost, though they don't seem to grieve
so much as mock, by strolling overhead,
where they evacuate, then leave.

He's fascinated by the globe they've made,
it stuns and soothes; no precatory shout
disturbs the buzz of the fly-quiet glade.
Sometimes he'll stand and watch its shadows move,
as what one seldom wants to think about
goes on and on in plain view all day long,
and marvel how, at just the right remove,
it sounds like human industry and song.

The Pursuit

I'm mountain ranges from my home
and heat is dancing up the road.
I can't recall what made me leave.
Was it a bur, a bar, a goad?

A wandering scholar sang your praise,
extolling stations on the way;
how steep the trail, I didn't ask,
how long the trek, he didn't say.

Unnumbered times I've cursed that bard
and damned each dark, abandoned shrine,
each woman who forbade a bed,
each inn where they refused me wine.

Contesting for my forward foot
distracted me from how I went;
better I never noticed that
the path began a slow ascent

until at last I felt you near,
like some pursuing, taunting elf.
I hurry on now, in a sweat
and keep my curses to myself.

Hymn Outside a Bank

Was it a stunting or a growth?
It was the risk of so much safety. It was both.
— Turner Cassity, "He Whom Ye Seek"

I can, although the branch on which it hangs is dead,
still make a brief obeisance at this ATM
and see through sea-green glass, as to an ocean bed,
the sort of deep in which you set the requiem.

A marbled dark where tellers, clerks and notaries
would tick the hours, while family trust and will reposed
in vaults, and customers could flock like votaries,
all free to doubt that any futures were foreclosed.

You wrote you went to one such place, that you were brisk
and (transubstantiation working as it must)
interred your poems, noting it involved some risk
to put your life to words, before the flesh was dust.

You never told how they were later resurrected;
like old Rossetti, you were silent as the grave.
But meditating on the wealth that you collected
replenishes the faith that, sometimes, verse can save.

Unawares, by Parrots

The sky erupts in rabid, bright green shrieking,
a bedlam which can only mean that harpies,
descending on the prey they've long been seeking,
have come to rend her to her very car keys,
right here—*of course*—in Target's parking lot.

But first—*as from some softer universe*—
they're going to send her mad, bereft of thought;
for what's that caterwaul, if not God's curse?
Mimesis (she conceives) *your name is parrot!*

She sees the tiny, arcing flocks that croak
across her line of sight; oh, how they share it
at no expense, their raucous cosmic joke,
in which they wink above, as she trails after

and watches fates fly off, to sounds like laughter.

Spinning Out

My son has Driver's Ed at Triple A
and I take auto courses on my own,
      parked and waiting here today,

retreading memories of cars I've known—
when a forgotten evening rumbles past
      from thirty-odd years back, then cuts in front,

momentum overtaking me so fast
that suddenly I'm running through a stunt
      I once performed in Paleolithic time

to learn how ancient Mustangs cornered: I'm
sixteen, a primitive jerk at unknown forces,
      and I, my car, and our unharnessed horses

go bungeeing around an unreal bend
I draw in air, but can't draw to an end
      till I've stopped sideways on a quiet road,

my lesson learned, no harm quite done.
From here, I can't tell more (had I forerun
      some curve to come in that old episode

or had a warning light switched on somehow?)
than that the turn still petrifies me now.

Dinner with the Smiths

For Jeanne Sloane

Tonight at La Goulue, the four of us,
out late the night before, are feeling dull.
We conjure old selves, who hold more of us
than do our current selves, to chase the lull.
As artisans might fashion figurines
to sounds of brightly clinking glass and tines,
we guide these antique selves through antic scenes
and polish them until each setting shines.
And then, to see us, basking and ensconced,
and laughing in our momentary bay—
the past re-catalogued and provenanced—
Jeanne, of a fine, appraising eye, might say,
it's for some future burnishing, as pleasant,
we give ourselves this gleaming, silver present.

November Flea Market

We've run a maze of outdoor market stalls,
racing as if to catch the last display,
the ultimate in old recycled ware—
a line of clouds above the mountains, where
a gold brocade is being drawn away.
More often, though, we've stopped
and lingered in the jumble, browsed for brass,
turned back to find each other, table-hopped
like ravens drawn by random bits of glass,
but though we've rushed or shopped,
we bought no time, and so the evening falls.

Those curios that light had animated
are blowing out; the leaden clouds drift west,
and chrome no longer signals from the tables.
A sour woman crates her orange crate labels:
Adios, California Dream, Hope Chest,
Cascade O' Gold, and Magic Isle
(Come back, O Persian Moon, shine overhead).
She adds the last two boxes to a pile
and gives a waiting van the go-ahead.

You catch her eye and smile;
how speedily our passing day gets freighted.
And standing on this playground of what was,
we watch as vendors straight from central casting
pack up a generation's worth of kitsch;

their aspects underscore that life's a bitch
and nothing, no, not nothing's everlasting.
Our picking's secondhand and scant,
and none of it endures or can be caught,
but then, the instant that I know it can't,
a joy that bounds horizons fills my thought—
faint as a dying chant—
It is enough, and has to do, and does.

After Sū San

Bed with you
is Mount Olympus
but now you've gone,
it's just White Plains again.

Gone Here

I have a memory
I can't identify,

slight and polychrome,
of some provisional room:

an entryway or hall
or sun-drowned vestibule.

The place is not important
for all of us are present.

We've come in with the light
or with it, drifting out,

are laughing and we're singing
and mightily arraying

or disrobing, in a globe
that, whirling, glints and strobes

with brightly streaming scarves
and hats like lofted leaves,

with sweaters, soft as nothing,
and coats with airy sleeves.

Just where or when this is,
or if it ever was,

who knows? The rest is gone.
It's us, as we were then,

no rude detail impinging
on our heroic changing.

The Switches

We felled the rotting tree before the rains,
fearing that it might crash through a wall,
but though the stump is all that still remains,
neither our home nor we were spared a fall
of less corporeal timber all around,
that fast collapse of structures at their roots
that brought uncounted households to the ground.

I've come to clear the stub, and find that shoots
have made a thin and yet resilient stand.
Observing them, I'm moved to think that we—
hit by a blow for which we hadn't planned
and severed from a vast old certainty—
like these few switches in a rough-made cleft,
may now go on to grow from what we've left.

We Go Without You

We go without you, since you're east at school,
and by the dim brick entryway we meet
more stranded parents in a humid pool
of mourners, damp with handkerchiefs and heat.

It's almost like old parents' nights inside,
though now with older parents in a queue.
We get the oldest children's course review
and greet the parents of the girl who died.

The lesson here is one we've always known:
you can be sheltered, loved, behave, do well,
and half a breath may blow it all to hell.
It's news we bury till the kids are grown.

We know we're wrong; it spells the overthrow
of our imperium when we presume
to spare you anything you ought to know.
Still, as I near the hollow in this room,

I'm bargaining to make the deal anew,
ransacking meager stores of grief and rage.
I lost my two loved parents to old age—
and fervently I wish that loss on you.

The Lath House

Wood strips, cross-purposed into lattice, made
this nursery of interstices—a place
that softened, then admitted, sun with shade,
baffled the wind and rain, broke open space.
It's now more skeletal, a ghostly room
the garden seemed to grow, in disrepair,
long empty and well past its final bloom.

Less lumbered, though, it cultivates the air
by shedding cedar slats for open sky.
As if, designed to never seem quite finished,
it had a choice to seal and stultify
or take its weather straight and undiminished,

grow larger but be less precisely here,
break with its elements, and disappear.

Refinishing Weather

With all of August crackled, baked, and hazed,
the prospect of observing paint congeal
or smoothing what a winter's damp had raised,
began to hold a certain warped appeal.

He lathed away those days this way, revealing
a depth that wasn't there beneath a surface
or mastering an art he'd use concealing
a flaw, then his technique, and then its purpose.

Some finishes are better not begun,
with others, luster quickly disappears,
and some, quite literally, are never done—
French polishing goes on and on, for years.

But, then, *re*-anything implies a loss,
a lack of permanence, an un-remaining.
Each burnished aniline's protective gloss
some day inevitably needs re-staining.

That didn't trouble him, the work felt good,
as when, in sanding down a table round,
his hands and paper whispered with the wood,
to shape an intricate, sustaining sound.

He was *refinishing*. He liked the way
the word proclaimed the task's utility
yet, looked at cool and clear, would still convey
a hand at faking and futility.

Afterword

Although the title of his fine collection of poems alludes to Giovanni Battista Tiepolo's *Triumph of Virtue and Nobility over Ignorance*, Frank Osen may put some readers in mind of a different exercise in visual allegory—Joshua Reynolds's *David Garrick Between Tragedy and Comedy*. Reading Osen, we can readily imagine him strolling amiably along, as Garrick does in Reynolds's portrait, with stately Melpomene on one arm and mischievous Thalia on the other. Like the famous actor, Osen in his poems enjoys celestial company and terrestrial experience alike, and he appears equally attracted to the two goddesses and to the genres of literature they represent. Judging from his writing, he is committed to serving them both and is happy to let them draw him, as they did Garrick, this way and that in their competition for his attention.

In any case, just as a dual allegiance to tragedy and comedy benefited Garrick's labors on the stage, so it has enriched Osen's poetry. Melpomene and Thalia have each inspired him to excellent poems. Moreover, Thalia's light grace has leavened the tragic ones, and Melpomene's seriousness has given weight to those of the funnier sort. For example, "Pacific Drift," which treats the mental deterioration and death of a parent, would not be nearly as effective as it is if Osen had not shaded and mitigated his grim topic by his quiet plays on words and by his well-sustained analogy between the instability of the California landscape and the precariousness of our footing on the planet. Similarly, in "Abstaining," which fancifully describes a body's senses and organs voting after a night of partying to give up liquor, Osen transcends the hilarity of the scene by communicating also the terrible resilience of appetite.

In his talent for tragedy and comedy, and for mixing them, Osen takes his place in a distinguished line of English-language poets that runs from Chaucer and Shakespeare down to our day. In some ways, Osen resembles those recent British masters of tragicomedy, Philip Larkin and Kingsley Amis. Indeed, he invokes the latter at one point in this collection. However, he is never as bilious as they sometimes are. He instead inclines to the less sharply satirical and more good-natured banter that we associate, rightly or wrongly, with American humor; and in this respect, he may remind us of another poet he refers to in this book, Wallace Stevens. Whether or not we agree with Osen's interpretation of "Mrs. Alfred Uruguay," he clearly appreciates Stevens's robust high-spiritedness. And we can recognize in Osen something of the Stevens who was not only a heartbreakingly perceptive student of mortality but also an incorrigible kidder—the Stevens who could in "Sunday Morning" write poignantly of death and yet who also could make his friend Margaret Powers roll on the floor with laughter at his droll account of a funeral he had lately attended.

Osen's poetry recalls as well that of Edwin Arlington Robinson. As does Robinson, Osen writes with some frequency about figures who struggle with a lopsided or thwarted genius or who find themselves hopelessly ill-adjusted to their world. Just as Robinson portrays time and again such fish-out-of-water characters as Miniver Cheevy and Eben Flood, so Osen appears fascinated by people whose lives have been dislocated or broken off by arbitrary fate. A moving poem of Osen's that expresses this interest is "Private School," which depicts a man who flees political tyranny in Argentina, only to find another (and in some ways even more degrading) form of brutality when he becomes a teacher of Spanish in a secondary school in the United States. And if Robinson's poems derive their power partly from the poet's modesty—from his never pretending to know more about his subjects than he does—Osen exhibits a similarly appealing self-critical or self-corrective spirit. For instance, after trenchantly judging, in "Reproof," a hot-rodder who killed himself and others by his reckless driving, Osen admits, in "Spinning Out," that he, too, has been prey to the same destructive impulses. Likewise, after having written tellingly, in "Pacific Drift," about a parent's death, he qualifies his grief in "We Go Without You." This latter poem acknowledges that nature itself decrees that the older generation should die before the younger does and that, as painful as it is to lose a parent, a child's death is, in its violation of natural order and promise, far more deeply anguishing.

Reynolds's portrait notwithstanding, David Garrick's greatest inspiration came from his wife, the dancer Eva Marie Veigel. As Osen's "Two-Person Ketch" and "After Sū San" indicate, his real muse is his wife Susan; and on the evidence of *Virtue, Big as Sin*, she is more than up to the role. Artists, however, need as much backup as they can get. Presently, Osen works in San Marino, California, at the Huntington Library. Though its art collections do not include *David Garrick Between Tragedy and Comedy*—that resides in the United Kingdom at Waddesdon Manor—the Huntington does have Reynolds's *Sarah Siddons as the Tragic Muse* and George Romney's *Emma Hart in a Straw Hat*. The poet who has made such an auspicious debut with this collection of poems is poised to move confidently forward on the basis of his own ample resources. But if he ever requires an energizing jolt, he can, it is cheering to reflect, petition the assistance of the commanding Mrs. Siddons and the sly, delightful Lady Hamilton. He is one of their company, and they look after their own.

—Timothy Steele

"Portrait of Alexis Piron [?]": Alexis Piron (1689-1773), French epigrammatist and playwright. The portrait, so labeled, by Louis Tocqué (1696-1772), once hung opposite Tiepolo's *Triumph of Virtue and Nobility Over Ignorance* and alongside Boucher's *Vertumnus and Pomona* in the Norton Simon museum; each of the paintings may be viewed on the museum's website.

"Private School": *Preguntas* (Questions) is a Spanish textbook.

"Cover Memo": The epigraph is from *The Collected Letters of Wallace Stevens,* Holly Stevens, ed. (New York: Alfred A. Knopf, 1966), p. 92.

"At the Dedication of von Weber's Monument in Dresden, October 11, 1860": *Der Freischütz (The Free-shot)* is considered the first important German Romantic opera. The hero, Max, uses magic bullets to win a shooting contest for his beloved Agatha, but the evil Zamiel guides the final bullet. Weber was ill when he travelled to London with his final opera, *Oberon,* in 1826. He died two weeks after its premiere, his death hastened by difficulties with the librettist, Planché. Eighteen years later, through the urging of Wagner and others, Weber's body was returned to Dresden. Details are found in *Enchanted Wanderer,* by Lucy Poate Stebbins and Richard Poate Stebbins (New York: G.P. Putnam's Sons, 1940).

"So Noble That . . .": No one, as far as I know, has yet interpreted it this way, but the Wallace Stevens poem is essentially a shaggy dog story of the sort the Hartford Accident and Indemnity Company's vice president might have told over martinis at the Canoe club. On riddles in Stevens's work, in general, see *Enigmas and Riddles in Literature,* by Eleanor Cook (Cambridge: Cambridge University Press, 2006), pp. 210-225.

"The Misfortunes of Juan Crisóstomo Jacobo Antonio de Arriaga y Balzola": Spanish composer (1806-1826). Details of the life are taken from *Arriaga, the Forgotten Genius: the Short Life of a Basque Composer,* by Barbara Rosen (Reno: Basque Studies Program, University of Nevada Press, 1988).

FRANK OSEN was born in Yokosuka, Japan, in 1954, grew up in Southern California, and is a graduate of the University of California at Berkeley and Loyola Law School in Los Angeles. He worked for many years in law, as general counsel to health care companies and also in real estate investment. He lives in Pasadena, California, and walks to work at the Huntington Library. He and his wife, Susan, have been married  for thirty years and have three grown children. *Virtue, Big as Sin* is his first full-length collection and the winner of the 2012 Able Muse Book Award.

Other Books from Able Muse Press

Ben Berman, *Strange Borderlands - Poems*

Michael Cantor, *Life in the Second Circle - Poems*

Catherine Chandler, *Lines of Flight - Poems*

Maryann Corbett, *Credo for the Checkout Line in Winter - Poems*

Margaret Ann Griffiths, *Grasshopper - The Poetry of M A Griffiths*

April Lindner, *This Bed Our Bodies Shaped - Poems*

Alexander Pepple (Editor), *Able Muse Anthology*

Alexander Pepple (Editor), *Able Muse - a review of poetry, prose & art*
 (semiannual issues, Winter 2010 onward)

James Pollock, *Sailing to Babylon - Poems*

Aaron Poochigian, *The Cosmic Purr - Poems*

Hollis Seamon, *Corporeality - Stories*

Matthew Buckley Smith, *Dirge for an Imaginary World - Poems*

Wendy Videlock, *The Dark Gnu and Other Poems*

Wendy Videlock, *Nevertheless - Poems*

Richard Wakefield, *A Vertical Mile - Poems*

www.ablemusepress.com

CPSIA information can be obtained at www.ICGtesting.com
Printed in the USA
LVOW08s2222260614

391961LV00005B/306/P